The Beauty of
SEOUL

Photographs by **SUH JAE-SIK**

HOLLYM
Elizabeth, NJ · Seoul

The Beauty of Seoul

First published in 2001
by Hollym International Corp.
18 Donald Place Elizabeth, New Jersey 07208, U.S.A.
Phone: (908)353-1655   Fax: (908)353-0255
http://www.hollym.com

Published simultaneously in Korea
by Hollym Corporation; Publishers
Core Bldg., 13-13 Kwanchol-dong, Chongno-gu
Seoul 110-111, Korea
Phone: (02)735-7551~4   Fax: (02)730-5149, 8192
http://www.hollym.co.kr   E-mail: hollym@cholian.net

ISBN: 1-56591-160-1
Library of Congress Catalog Card Number: 2001091319

Printed in Korea by Samsung Moonwha Printing Co., Ltd.
Phone: (02)468-0361~5   Fax: (02)461-6798

Bound in Korea by Myung Ji Mun Hwa Co., Ltd.
Phone: (02)858-0101~9   Fax: (02)858-0100

CONTENTS

Introduction

Seoul is an international megalopolis with a population of well over 10 million. Among the most prestigious buildings in the city is Sungnyemun (South Gate), National Treasure No. 1. Around the ancient gate cars congest the area that once led to the old city. Visitors to the city soon recognize that downtown Seoul is a city that accomodates both tradition and modernity.

Over 600 years has passed since Yi Seonggye, King Taejo (founder) of Joseon Dynasty passed through the gate to the new capital Hanyang (currently Seoul) from Gaegyeong. The economic "Miracle of the Hangang River" began in the 1960's when Korea began exporting its products to numerous foreign countries. With brisk economic activity, Korea is a country filled with great energy and vitality. Koreans defeated the cold IMF waves, and have started a new millennium.

Korea is no longer the poor and undeveloped country it used to be. The Seoul Olympics was successfully held in 1988. The 3rd ASEM Summit Conference was held in October 2000 at the Convention Center at Samseong-dong, Gangnam-gu, and the World Cup Games will be held in Seoul in 2002. The ASEM conference helped Korea with cultural and other tourist development. As with the Olympic games in 1988, Seoul will become more internationally known because of the 2002 World Cup Games and international art festivals.

The Olympic Highway runs 36km along the Hangang River under the bright lights and radiant fireworks.

Seoul, a sprawling International city, has a population of over 10 million people.

Olympic Town which accomodated the athletes during the Games of the XXIVth Olympiad 1988. Juan Antonio Samaranch, President of the International Olympic Committee said, "Seoul toward the World, the World toward Seoul" to a crowd of 100,000 people and 13,600 athletes at the opening ceremory of Seoul Olympiad.

Seoul Through Trial and Change

Primitive people of the Hangang River, 6000 years ago.

In the old Silla Dynasty people called the capital city "Seobeol," "Seorabeol,"or "Saebeol". In the Joseon Dynasty people wrote "Seowon" and pronounced it "Seoul". Seoul was officially renamed in 1945. Seoul itself means capital city. Today Seoul symbolizes the Republic of Korea.

Located in the west central part of the Korean Peninsula, Seoul is surrounded by many mountains. Among the world's large cities there are few with as many mountains as Seoul. The Hangang river flows from east to west through the heart of the city. The river is wider than the Seine of Paris, the Thames of London, and the Rhein of Bonn. The widest part of river is 1.5 km and the narrowest is 50 m.

It is assumed that men were living in the Seoul area along the lower reaches of the Hangang River in the Paleolithic Age. Archaeological remains and relics attest to the fact that people already began to lead settled lives here in the Neolithic Age. The prehistoric remains unearthed in Amsa-dong, Gangdong-gu date back to the Neolithic Age of about 6,000 years ago.

It was not until the early Three Kingdoms period, however, that the Seoul area became well inhabited and developed into collective dwelling sites. The Baekje Kingdom was founded in 18 B.C. by Onjo, believed to be the son of Jumong of Goguryeo, with its capital at Habuk Wirye Castle north of the Hangang River. The Hangang River area was the battle ground of the three kingdoms; Silla, Goguryeo, and Baekje. At present Garak-dong, Seokchon-dong, Bangee-dong, Achasanseong, Pungnabtoseong and Mongchontoseong are the historic sites of the Baekje Kingdom.

During the Goryeo Dynasty, Hanyang, Seogyeong (present Pyeongyang) and Donggyeong (present Gyeongju) were three designated capitals. These cities were chosen as capitals by the government in accordance with the geomantic theory known as *pungsujiri* (literally, the theory of wind and water) of the geographic philosophy of the Orient.

According to Yi Seonggye in *The History of Seoul*, King Taejo of the Joseon Dynasty began a new State in February 1392. He decided to move to the new capital to seek political stability under a renewed spirit and to win people's support. The front site of Mt. Bukhansan was chosen for the new seat of the government which encompassed the oriental geomantic theory. In October 28, A.D. 1394, King Taejo settled in Hanyang. He began to construct the Royal Ancestral shrines, Altars and Gyeongbokgung Palace. Since that time Seoul has been the capital city of Korea. Gyeongseong, the name used for the city by the Japanese, was renamed Seoul in 1945 after National Liberation. Seoul was separated from Gyeonggi-do Province and became officially the city of Seoul in August 1949.

After the Korean war Seoul was rebuilt and developed into a modern city. High buildings and tall apartment complexes were built all over the city. 60 percent of Korean banks, business headquarters, and a lot of well-known universities are situated in Seoul.

In 1988 the 24th Summer Olympic Games was held in Seoul with 160 countries participating. The 3rd ASEM Summit was held at Samsung Convention Center in October, 2000 which was the biggest international conference ever held in Seoul history. The 2002 World Cup Games will be held in Seoul and other cities both in Korea and Japan. Seoul will continue to achieve well-balanced development in the 21st century.

Prehistoric Remains

In 1967 the prehistoric remains unearthed at Amsa-dong, Gangdong-gu date back to the Neolithic Age of about 6,000 years ago. 28 original house sites, earthenware and stoneware were discovered, and some of them are included in the 9 replicas.

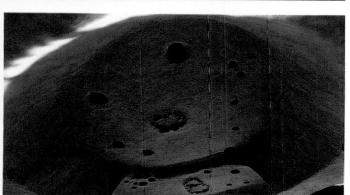

The Mt. Bukhansan Monument

Silla entered into an alliance with King Seong of Baekje in 551 to drive out the Goguryeo forces, taking 10 counties along the upper reaches of the Hangang River and expanding further toward the lower reaches of the Hangang River. The King Jinheung of Silla took control of the areas around the Hangang River within two years. He toured around the newly taken territory and set up monuments to commemorate his conquest. The Mt. Bukhansan Monument on top of the Bi-bong Peak was erected in the 16th year of King Jinheung's reign (above).

On National Liberation Day in August, 1945, Gyeongseong was renamed "Seoul," capital city of Korea (right).

The Korean War

The Korean War broke out on June 25, 1950. The city was devastated by the war. But soon after the war the city was rebuilt and developed into a megalopolis.

Seoul is a world megalopolis. It accomodates tradition and modernity.

Seoul Opens the New Millennium

Seoul is a sprawling international city with a population of more than 10 million. It is the fifth largest city in the world. Seoul has a population density of 18,000 people per 2km, which makes it one of the most densely populated countries in the world. Seoul is 605.52 km², which is 6 % of Korea's total land area. Twenty-five percent of Korea's population lives in Seoul. Of every 4 people in Korea one lives in Seoul.

Since 1394 Seoul has been the symbolic and functional capital city of Korea for 600 years. But the country has had to overcome many difficult periods, such as foreign invasions, the Japanese occupation, and the Korean War. From a political, economical, educational, and cultural stand point, Seoul is a leader of cities. Korea's economic might derives from the economic power of Seoul. The average traffic population a day is 26 million. Of the 28 percent of all motor vehicles in the country, 1.65 million are in Seoul. On average private cars move 22.9 km an hour. The speed of the traffic is similar to a marathoner's running speed. The subway train system started in 1974 and is becoming a more popular mode of transportation. By using the subway people can move two to four times faster than private cars.

With a view to solving both problems of population concentration and the housing land shortage, the central government created large-scale apartment communities in outer regions of the city. Satelite cities in Seongnam-si and in Goyang-si have been built around the capital successfully to help ease mounting pressure from the shortage of housing.

Around Myeong-dong and Sogong-dong which represent commerical areas there are many leading department stores and shoes shops. People crowd these areas day and night. In the evening brilliant neon signs make the area bright and enticing. These are the most advanced fashion centers, and they offer a variety of street festivities every year.

Itaewon is a well known shopping area for foreigners. The presence of the U.S. military base turned the street into an "international area" from the post-Korean war. An increasing number of foreign tourists visit this area because of its wide range of bargains plus a host of English-speaking shop owners. The main street has really become one of the most famous shopping paradises in Seoul.

400,000 foreign travellers visit Seoul every month, and among them 250,000 travellers individually visit Seoul. They travel around Seoul and its vicinities for two or three days to shop and sightsee. Recently Seoul city tour buses have been introduced in the city. Authorized by the Seoul Metropolitan Government, the buses provide a safe and convenient way to see the city. All the sights and attractions of Seoul can be seen on one tour. In the daytime the bus stops by Deoksugung Palace, Itaewon, and at night it stops at the National Theater, and the Seoul Tower at Mt. Namsan. The bus stops at about 20 different sightseeing attractions throughout the city.

Seoul has developed in accordance with the long term economic plan started in the 1960's into a truly international metropolis. The newly opened Incheon International Airport functions as a hub for Northeast Asia in this new century of information and technology.

Located in the west central part of the Korean Peninsula, Seoul lies at the 126° 59' east longitude and 37° 34' north latitude. Korea has four distinct seasons. Summer is the monsoon season. On a clear autumn day, the city's panoramic view is breathtaking.

Sungnyemun Gate (Namdaemun Gate) is a 600-year old wooden structure in Seoul. Its grand scale and elegant design is one of its outstanding features. It is National Treasure No. 1 (far left). At Seoul Tower, Mt. Namsan you can see the Incheon sea through a telescope on clear days (above). Jongno Tower is the most modern architectural masterpiece in Seoul (left). It received the Grand Prix for Architecture from the Seoul Metropolitan Government.

No vehicles at Sejongno Street. The Seoul Metropolitan Government designated special days when no vehicles are allowed at Sejongno Street. On that day citizens can walk to Gwangwhamun Gate at their leisure.

The Millennium Festival was officially held by the Seoul Metropolitan Government at many places in Seoul. Over 100,000 people participated in the festival.

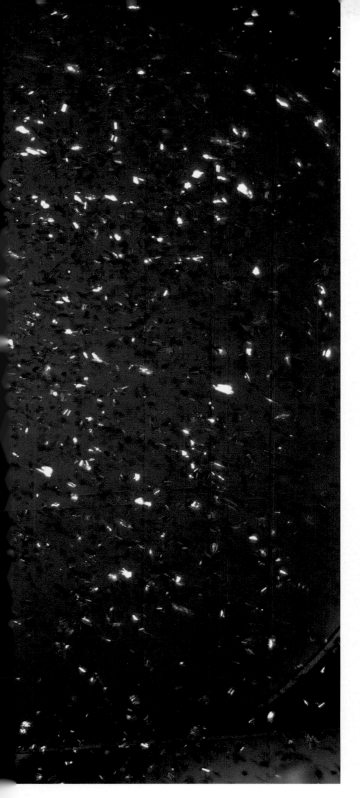

Yi Seonggye, King Taejo of Joseon Dynasty relocated the capital city to Hanyang (Seoul) in 1394. The Seoul Metropolitan Government has designated October 28 as Seoul Citizen's Day to commemorate the 600th anniversary of relocating the capital city.

Seoul Citizen's Day festivals are becoming familiar to all citizens living in Seoul. At Jongno and Sejongno about 10,000 people gather to celebrate the festive day. They hold many different types of events and parades (right and above).

Yeouido Public Park

Another city within the city is Yeouido (pp.41-42). Yeouido is the center of politics and finance. It is home to the National Assembly, the financial district, the mass media networks and large banks.
On weekdays, office workers eat lunch at the numerous restaurants available in the area. On weekends, people enjoy bicycle riding, roller skating, and DDR in the vast recreational plaza (this page and far left).

The Seoul Metropolitan Government made Yeouido Plaza into a public park to expand the resort area for citizens. There is a 2.8 km bicycle road, a jogging course, an outdoor music hall, an octagon area, and a Korean traditional pond.

Yeouido is over 900 thousand 'pyeong'(one pyeong is 400/121m²). The 63 Building which is the highest building in Korea commands a majestic view of Seoul.

Itaewon; Shopping Paradise

Itaewon is crowded with 2,000 stores including shops that sell shoes, clothes, and bags. Restaurants, specializing in various ethnic foods, are also located conveniently along the main shopping street. It is a venue for many foreign tourists in Korea.

Itaewon is a well known shopping area to foreigners. During the 2002 World Cup Games thousands of foreigners will visit the area. The main street has become one of the most famous shopping paradises in Korea.

Insa-dong; A Hub of Tradition and Culture

Insa-dong is the hub of tradition and culture. It is crowded with stores selling ceramics, old paintings, wood items, brassware and many other relics of the past. Visitors can get a glimpse of Korea's cultural heritage with its many ancient antiques from the Silla Dynasty to the Joseon Dynasty displayed side by side. It also has a wide variety of cuisine from around the world.

Insa-dong is a must for those who want to understand authentic Korean ambience. Its street, are packed with art galleries, antique shops, ceramics shops, and Korean restaurants. It is called a 'living cultural treasure' and a must visit 'street museum'.

Myeong-dong; A Variety of Specialty Stores

Often called a 'shopping paradise', the Myeong-dong area is lined with upscale shopping malls and department stores as well as a variety of specialty stores.

Apgujeong-dong; The Myeong-dong of Gangnam

Apgujeong-dong is called the Myeong-dong of Gangnam. If you have only a day in town and want to dive head first into the modern Korean phenomenon, this sprawling upscale district is the place to go. It's a thriving neighborhood and you'll never run out of things to explore.

Dongdaemun Market; World Fashion

Dongdaemun Market is a shopping Mecca for today's new fashion conscious generation.
Talented young designers, sensitive to world fashion trends, make sure that new sensations making their debut on the Paris runways show up at Dongdaemun Market the very next day.
Led by the fashion houses of Doosan Tower, Freya Town, Uno Core, and Migliore, the market attracts thousands of shoppers daily.

61

Namdaemun Market; A Traditional Market

Adjacent to Namdaemun (South Gate) is the Namdaemun Market, one of the largest traditional outdoor markets in Seoul. Retailers from across the nation flock to these stores. Many foreigners buy clothes at 30-40% discount prices.

There are shopping guides for foreigners at Namdaemun market. Buyers and sellers buy and sell merchandise from midnight to 4 a.m. The market is packed with hundreds of shops and stalls full of a wonderful variety of merchandise at a low price you can afford.

Dongsung-dong Daehangno is called 'youth street', 'theater street', and 'cultural street' because its neighborhood encompasses various places for visitors to amuse themselves and pass the time, such as cafes, galleries, theaters and peformance halls.

Lotte World is the largest complex in Seoul where an indoor theme park, an outdoor park by a lake are situated. Characters wear traditional costumes from around the world and perform folk dances to a captivated audience. The world carnival is shown twice a day.

Lotte World; World Carnival Parade

The giant Lotte World complex is an exciting and enjoyable place to spend a couple of days for recreation and diversion. The Folk Museum is worth a visit. Lotte World is a world of magic, fantasy and adventure.

COEX; Center of International Trade

The 3rd ASEM conference was held at Samsung Convention Center. The center consists of 11 Exhibition Halls and 56 conference rooms. It is an augury of prosperity and stability in the New Millennium. Twenty six summits from Asia and Europe met at the COEX (Convention and Exhibition) center in October 2000.

When you walk through the tunnel at the COEX Aquarium, it feels as if you are walking under the sea.

Designed with every possible convenience in mind, the COEX center accommodates conventioneers who would like to stop for clothes in one of the many clothing stores. Situated nearby is the city airport terminal which offers direct limousine service to Incheon Airport. COEX functions as the center of international trade and cultural exchange in the 21st century.

Art Exhibitions in Subway Trains

In many of the subway trains, famous paintings are on display for the passengers to enjoy.
You can also enjoy musical, performances, and fashion shows.

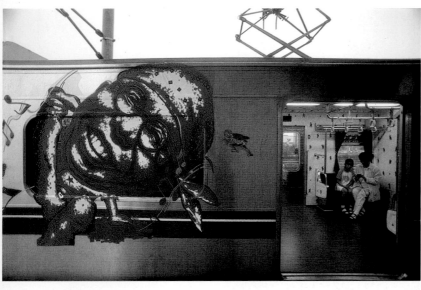

Some of Seoul subway stations have become new stages of culture and art. Millions of people can enjoy music and fine art at the subway station.

Seoul Media City

World Image art makes Seoul a media city. The main theme is "Seoul City between 0 and 1". Seoul has become a new net city beyond the limit of time and space. Citizens enjoy media art even in the street. The Seoul World Culture Festival is to be held every other year. The Biennial International Multimedia Show fuses science and new technologies with fine art.

Computer and Internet

Computers reduce the distance of time and space. The internet manages to work effectively all over the world.

Computers make it easier to conduct business. We can talk face to face using distant image systems. At home, the computer manages home banking, and home shopping. Daily life has become much more efficient and convenient.

Seoul is in a pleasant city to live in. The long-term plan to improve the quality of the air and water will help bring Seoulites and visitors a higher quality of living.

Seoul has achieved balanced and sustainable development. To preserve Seoul's natural areas, Seoul citizens have tried to keep construction to a minimum. Most apartment complexes have large green areas.

The Quality of Korean Beef 'Galbi'

To broil beef ribs (galbi) on charcoal is one of the best ways to taste top quality Korean beef and is one of Korea's favorite dishes. To broil beef on the chacoal is to keep the original taste.

Seoul Arts Center

The Seoul Arts Center houses the Opera House, the first of its kind in Asia, and the 'Towol' Theater mainly for the performance of Korean traditional dramas. The Center also houses the Seoul Concert Hall, the Art Research Hall, the Calligraphy Hall, the Hangaram Fine Art Exhibition Hall and the National Institute of Korean Traditional Music.

The Seoul Arts Center is the only facility of its kind in Asia. The Sejong Cultural Center has been the main stage for symphonies, concerts, operas and ballets of the highest international caliber as well as a host of Korean traditional folk performances.

"Grand Concert of Drums and Dancing": all types of drums are used in the percussion festival.

Majestic and elegant traditional court dance. The motion of the dance is very slow and soft which was handed down from ancient times.

The *Hakmu* Dance (Crane Dance) was handed down from Goryeo Dynasty which includes the *Cheoyongmu* Dance, and the *Sadaedogam*. The *Hakmu* Dance, the *Yeonwhadaemu* Dance, and the *Cheoyong* became the *Hakyeonwha Daesunmu* Dance.

Bongsan talchum (Bongsan Mask Dance)

Bongsan talchum (Bongsan Mask Dance) is satirical and humorous. With a light motion, the dancer's arms slowly stretch to the rythym of the music. The dance originated in Bongsan, Hwanghae-do Province. People performed it on Dano Day in May and on Chuseok Day in August at the market plaza or Gyeonganru yard from evening to dawn. Human heritage performer Kim Gi-su performs a praying ritual scene just before beginning the dance.

Museums in Seoul

There are 73 museums and art galleries in Seoul. Nine of them, including the National Museum of Korea, are national or public museums. National Treasure No. 92, *Cheongdong Eunibsaporyu Sugeummunjeongbyeong* (Bronze vase with willow and fowl designs inlaid in silver; above) is exquisite, and elegant. It is a 1,000 year-old cultural heritage.

Trees, flowers, birds and breathing fish, combine harmoniously. *Buncheonsagi* and *Goryeocheongja* are fine and elegant ancienct ceramic vases.

The acting elderly ministers who participate in the Royal procession of Joseon Dynasty get together before Myeongjeongmun Gate, Changgyeonggung Palace. The colors of their uniforms are red, blue, or green according to their rank.

Old Palaces of the Joseon Dynasty

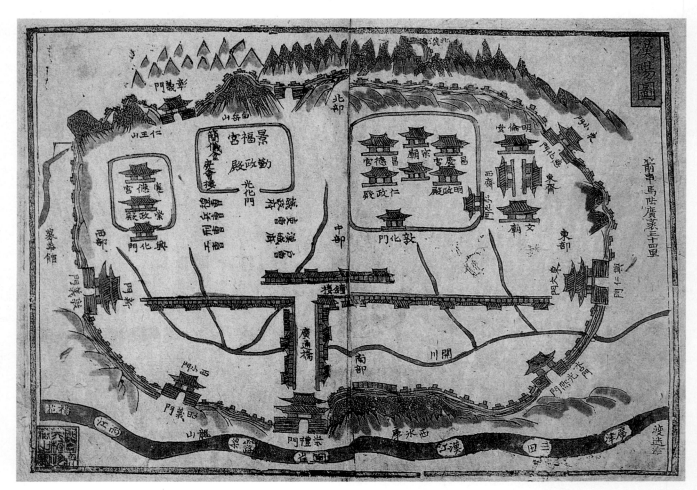

Hanyang(Seoul) Map made about 1770. The wall around Hanyang is about 17 km.

Inside the old palaces of the Joseon Dynasty, you feel as if you are in the peaceful mountains. In the shady grove and nearby streams you can experience tranquillity and feel deep seclusion. The quiet atmosphere of the palaces contrasts with the high buildings and noise outside of the palaces.

The five representative palaces of Joseon Dynasty are Gyeongbokgung Palace, Changdeokgung Palace, Changgyeonggung Palace, Deoksugung Palace and Gyeonghuigung Palace. The first palace, Gyeongbok-gung Palace was constructed in 1395 right after the founding of Joseon Dynasty by King Taejo. The palace was burned down during the Japanese Hideyoshi Invasions and the current palace was rebuilt by the Prince Regent Daewon in 1868.

Changdeokgung Palace was originally built in 1405. It houses the Injeongjeon (audience hall) which has been designated as a National Treasure No. 225. There is a beautifully landscaped Secret Garden with numerous reception rooms, pavilions and gates, such as the Yeonghwadang, Chundangdae, and Soyo-jeong.

Changgyeonggung Palace was built by King Seongjong for the queen's grandmother, mother, and aunt. It was built by adding several buildings to the former Palace of Suganggung, which had been built by King Sejong for his aging father, King Taejong. The Honghwamun is the main gate of the palace.

Deoksugung Palace, situated in the heart of Seoul, is just in front of City Hall. It was originally a private residence for Prince Wolsan, the elder brother of King Seongjong. King Seonjo once took up residence there when Gyeongbokgung Palace and Chang-deokgung Palace were burned down during the Japanese Hideyoshi Invasion in 1592. King Seonjo lived there for 16 years. The Emperor Gojong also stayed there after the Empress Myeongseong's death. Because Gyeonghuigung Palace is situated west of Gyeongbokgung Palace, it was called West Palace. It was large and majestic. A big fire in 1829 burned down the palace.

Jongmyo is the royal ancestral shrine which was designated as a World Cultural Heritage by UNESCO in 1995. It houses the tablets of kings and queens and offer sacrifices to the ancestors of the royal family. Jongmyo is the symbol of the Joseon Dynasty together with the Sajikdan, an altar where sacrifices were offered to the gods of earth and grains. Jongmyo consists of Jeongjeon, the main shrine, and Yeongnyeongjeon, a separate shrine.

Unhyeongung was the residence of the royal family. The 26th King Gojong was born there and lived there until he was 12. Later it became a royal descendant Yi Haeung's (1820-90) residence.

The Mt. Namsan area in Jung-gu District has many replicas of old tiled traditional Korean-style houses called 'Hanok'. The Korean style houses are slowly being replaced by western style houses. Modern apartment complexes have already become the common form of housing in Seoul.

Changdeokgung Palace

Changdeokgung Palace was first built as a detached extension to the main Gyeongbokgung Palace by King Taejong the third monarch of the Joseon Dynasty. From King Gwanghae to King Gojong, spanning a period of about 300 years, this was the main residence for all monarchs during their reigns.

The royal garden of Changdeokgung Palace is located to the rear of the palace with rare trees and flowers found everywhere along the grounds of the palace. This beautiful palace best represents the beauty, taste, and skill of Korean craftsmanship. The fan shaped Gwanllamjeong of the peninsular pond (above). Aeryeonjeong surrounded by beauty of late autumn (left).

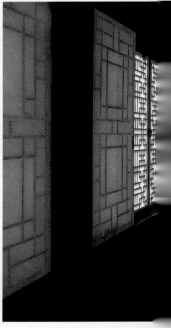

Nakseonjae and Manwolmun Gate

Full moon-shaped Manwolmun Gate of Nakseonjae in Changdeok-gung Palace was originally a retreat where queens used to stay during the royal family mourning period. It is the reason why the house is modestly decorated. But later the Kings' beloved palace ladies lived there and the house was beautifully painted and decorated.

The Flower Garden which is one of the most beautiful places in Nakseonjae.
Through all the seasons we can enjoy the beautiful and green grass and
trees.

Suganggung Palace became Changgyeonggung Palace

Changgyeonggung Palace was originally built in 1419 and named Suganggung Palace by King Sejong as a residential palace for his predecessor King Taejong. Later the palace became the main Royal palace of King Seongjong and the name was subsequently changed to Changgyeonggung Palace in the 15th year of his reign.

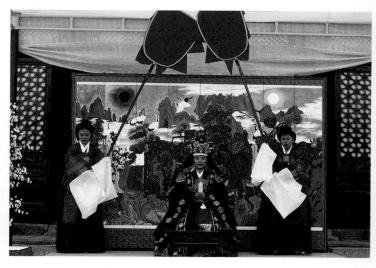

Gwageo (state examination) of Goryeo Dynasty was carried over into the Joseon Dynasty. The examination system continued for one thousand years from the beginning of Goryeo Dynasty to the end of the Joseon Dynasty. The examination was one of the important state policies.

Geunjeongjeon Pavilion, National Treasure No. 224 of Joseon Dynasty was built near the Square Pond inside Gyeonghoeru. Kings held banquets at the pavilion on special occasions.

Gyeongbokgung Palace;
The Main Palace of Joseon Dynasty

Gyeongbokgung Palace was built in 1395 as a residence for the royal family of the Joseon Dynasty. It was the main palace of the Kingdom. It was burned down during the Japanese Invasion in 1592, but was later rebuilt. The rear garden, Amisan, is a representative traditional Korean garden. The trees change their colors every season (above right). Hyangwonjeong Pavilion was full of the fragrance of lotus flowers (below right).

The Joseon Dynasty is still visible in every corner of Seoul. The Joseon Dynasty palaces make Seoul truly a city of palaces.

The flowered wall of Jagyeongjeon in Gyeongbokgung Palace is finely patterned. The wall is patterned with pine, bamboo, orchids, and chrysanthemums. Other walls are patterned with deers, cranes, turtles, sun, moon, and waterfalls. The walls often stood for people's social status.

A winter of snow covers Hyangwonjeong Pavilion. The Kings used to invite scholars and famous people to sit on the pavilion and enjoy the beautiful garden with them.

Jongmyo; The Royal Ancestral Shrine

Jongmyo is the royal ancestral shrine which was designated as a World Cultural Heritage by UNESCO in 1995. Even though it is in the congested downtown area, inside the shrine is calm and peaceful.

Jongmyojerye and Jeonju Yi Family

Jongmyodaeje is Important Intangible Cultural Property No. 56. Sacrifices to the ancestors of the royal family were held here four times a year. Recently the rite, presented according to a set of traditional rules on the first Sunday of May, is a yearly memorial service for the royal ancestors of Joseon Dynasty. 64 people dance the *parilmu* (a traditional dance).

Jongmyojerye and Jongmyojeryeak were designated as World Heritage. This is the first time that the intangible cultural properties are registered in the World Heritage list of the UNESCO.

Jongmyojerye consists of music and dance. The music is for the rites of the royal ancestors. The dance is called *Parilmu* which is performed only for the Emperor's Rite. The dance consists of *Munmu* and *Mumu*. To dance *Munmu*, the dancer holds a long flute in the left hand, and a short flute made of pheasant feathers in the right hand. To dance *Mumu* the dancers hold a wooden spear and wooden sword.

Jongmyojerye was revived under the auspices of the Jeonju Yi family who are the descendants of Joseon Dynasty. The Rite is presented according to a set of traditional rules.

The peaceful Jongmyojerye, accompanying the process of the rite, is distinguished historically and artistically by its meaningful message. The officials receive a tripod wine cup and a bowl and then partake in a sacrificial drink. At the end, all participants step down the terrace and offer four deep bows.

Deoksugung Palace and Emperor Gojong

Situated right in the heart of Seoul, just in front of City Hall, Deoksugung Palace was a private residence for prince Wolsan, an elder brother of King Seongjong. King Seonjo, however, once took up residence here when Gyeongbokgung Palace and Changdeokgung Palace were burned during the Japanese Invasion. The Emperor Gojong also stayed here after the Empress Myeongseong's death.

Deoksugung Palace is a place that serves as a reminder of so many bad memories in Korean history that it was once slated to be destroyed.

Fortunately, this palace has been restored to its original glory and opened to the public. It is a quiet resort in a noisy city.

The Royal Guards Changing Ceremony

The Royal Guards Changing Ceremony is presented at the grand entrance to Deoksugung Palace in the afternoon. The guards wear traditional military uniforms and swords. This ceremony attracts many foreigners and it is one of the famous events in Seoul.

Jinchanyeon; A Big Banquet

Jinchanyeon held at the palace of the Joseon Dynasty is a congratulatory banquet for Kings or Queen's birthdays. Wine and special meals were provided with dance and music.

Jinchanyeon is the heart of palace culture. It shows the Korean traditional character of fidelity. Palace music, dance, meals, and clothes are used for the congratulatory events of King's or Queen's birthdays, especially 60th, 70th, or 80th birthdays.

Jinchanyeon table setting. Cho Haeng-ja who is a disciple of Intangible Cultural Property Cho Ok-wha set this table. On the table there are about 100 different meals that took one week to prepare.

When wine, dancing, and singing are offered the banquet reaches a climax at *Jinchanyeon*. The words of the song are "Cheers for longevity, live 100 thousand years for each glass of wine, live until 30,000 years old."

Royal Wedding at Unhyeongung Palace

Unhyeongung Palace was the residence of Prince Regent Heungseon Daewongun, who was the father of King Gojong, the 26th monarch of the Joseon Dynasty. King Gojong married Queen Myeongseong at Unhyeongung Palace. A royal wedding was a very important occasion.

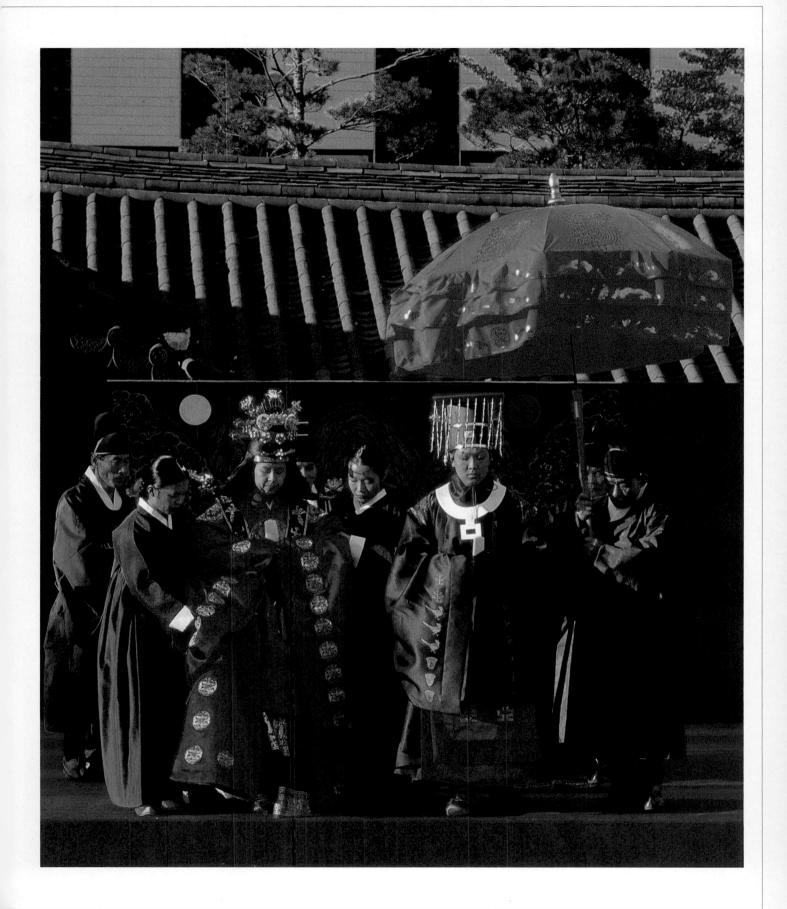

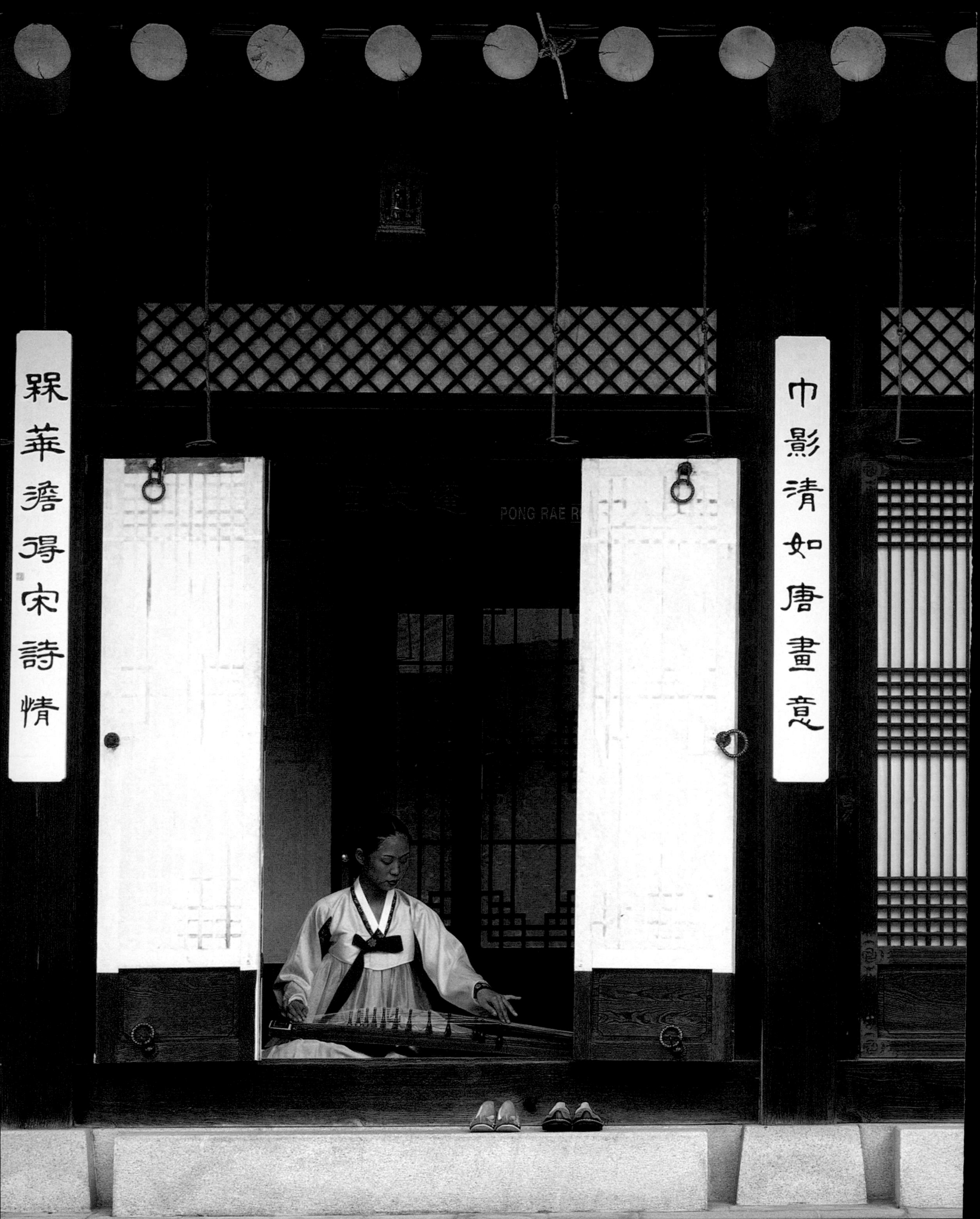
槑華澹得宋詩情
巾影清如唐畫意

醉眼看花紅漾繡

Korea House

Korea House introduces you to Korean traditional architecture, Korean daily life, performance arts, table settings, Korean wedding ceremony and various other Korean traditions. Korea House also provides authentic Korean cuisine with traditional dance and music every evening.

Though Korea House is downtown, the inside is very quiet. You can enjoy the scenes and sounds of nature. The house provides visitors a view of Korean sentiment and taste.

Korea House has a 170-seat folk theater where traditional fan dances, mask dances, and *Samulnori* are performed.

Namsangol Traditional Korean Village

Covering a site of 7,934 square meters at the northern tip of Mt. Namsan, the Namsangol Traditional Korean Village contains several units of classic style Hanok, or traditional Korean Houses. They were moved from their original locations scattered around the city in 1977. One of them is Yi Seung-eop House which was built in 1860.

Visitors to the Traditional Korean village can appreciate not only the living style of the *Yangban* or the aristocratic class of the Joseon Dynasty, but also traditional performances as well.

At the traditional Korean village we can witness the whole cycle of living. A child at a 1st Birthday party (far left). Jumping on wooden see-saw (left). *Nong-ak nori* that wishes a year of abundance (below left).
Korean traditional wedding and funeral ceremony (this page above and below).

Korean Traditional Knots Human Cultural Property, Kim Eun-young, demonstrates weaving
Korean traditional knots.

In Korea there are 24 artifacts fields. The Korean traditional knot is one of them. Knots originated in the Neolithic Age. The knots on these pages were woven by Human Cultural Property, Kim Eun-young.

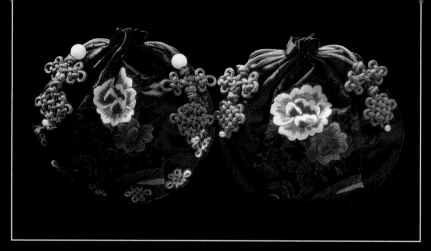

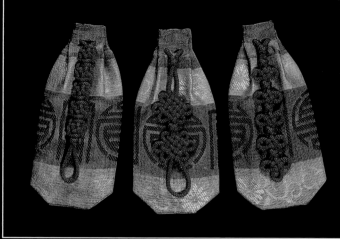

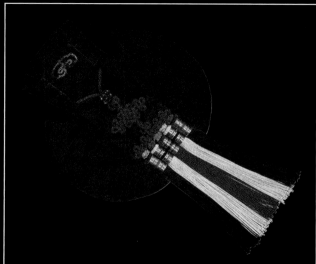

Norigae is different in form and meaning from other knots. For example, the triangle means heaven, earth, and man. The Chinese letter *Bok*(福) means happiness, *Su*(壽) longevity, *Gwi*(貴) noblity. The square, circle, butterfly, flower and dragon are typical patterns.

Hanok Village has been carefully designed to enable visitors to get a sense of the atmosphere as well as learn about the lifestyle and customs of life during the Joseon Dynasty. At an inner chamber two women are sewing (left). Two women are beating, *Dadeumijil* (below).

Mt. Bukhansan

The highest among the mountains surrounding Seoul is Mt. Bukhansan. It rises high behind Gyeongbokgung Palace. Mt. Bukhansan is also referred to as Mt. Samgaksan which means triangular mountain, because of the three conspicuous peaks of Baegundae, Insubong, and Mangyeongdae Peaks. Of the peaks, Insubong Peak is 250 meters high with a granite wall. Mountaineers like to climb this wall of granite.

Mt. Bukhansan (836m) is made of granite. The valley below is beautiful and has well preserved forests. The mountain has a long history and many legends.

In the past year, a few climbers have lost their lives climbing the popular mountain. But residents of Seoul love to frequent the mountain to rest and study nature. A climber is climbing Insubong Peak (left). A stream flows between rocks (above).

The fortress of Seoul is a valuable cultural property as well as a spiritual bond (above).
A snowy Insubong Peak at Mt. Bukhansan (right).

The Hangang River;
Seoul Citizen's Resort

At the Hangang River Seoul citizens' resort, many people gather to enjoy the many recreational activities.

The Hangang River flows through the central part of the Korean peninsula. The river spans a total of 497.5 kms, the fourth longest in Korea after the Yalu River, Dumangang River, and Nakdonggang River. The Hangang River combines the Namhangang River and the Bukhangang River. The Namhangang River starts from Mt. Taebaeksan, and the Bukhangang River starts from Mt. Geumgangsan. The two rivers merge at Yangsuri. The river accounts for about a third of the total water supply in Korea for both households and industry. The Hangang River flows through the city from east to west and lots of tributaries flow into it.

The river divides Seoul into two areas, Gangbuk and Gangnam. The river is seriously polluted due to Korea's rapid period of industrialization known as 'the Miracle of the Hangang River.' A comprehensive development project to clean up the river is currently underway.

Along the banks of the river, sewage treatment plants and drainage tunnels were constructed as well as city highways, including the Olympic Express which extends over 40 kms from the Haengju Bridge to the Misari area. Thirteen riverside parks stretching over six million square meters contain a full range of sport facilities, including fishing spots, water skiing and wind surfing facilities, and yacht moorages. In addition, modern pleasure ferries, several of which have varying double-decker designs, ply the river between four piers. All the leisure facilities are easily accessible, allowing citizens to enjoy outdoor sports and other pastimes all year round in this recovered natural area.

The riverside parks have seven sports plazas with various training facilities such as soccer fields, jogging tracks, roller skating lanes, bicycle lanes, outdoor swimming pools and other game areas. Each park has a spacious grassland for festive events for all seasons, such as kite-flying. The first bridge across the Hangang River was constructed in July, 1900; at present there are 27 bridges for motor vehicles and trains.

Seoul is situated on the lower reaches of the Hangang River which flows through the central part of the Korean pennisula. The Hangang River spans a total of 497.5 kms. Riverside park stretching out some 6,000,000 square meters contains a full range of sports facilities, including fishing spots, water skiing and wind surfing facilities.

The Hangang River

On the Hangang River modern pleasure ferries, several of which have varying double decker designs, ply the river between four piers.

The Hangang River leisure facilities are easily accessible, allowing citizens to enjoy outdoor sports and other pastimes all year round in this recovered natural environment.

Riverside park is installed with various physical training facilities such as soccer fields, jogging tracks, roller skating lanes, bicycle lanes, outdoor swimming pools and other game areas.

Many people enjoy swimming in one of the many swimming pools along the Hangang River. Especially in July and August people spend hot summer days at the swimming pools in Riverside park.

Beautiful lanterns embroider the Hangang River. Riverside park has spacious grass areas for festive events held during the seasons.

Lights illuminate the Grand Cheongdam Bridge that crosses the Hangang River.

The firework festival at Yeouido brightens the evening sky.

The 2002 World Cup Games

The 2002 World Cup Games will be held in major cities both in Korea and Japan. A 60,000-seat main stadium for the opening ceremony of the 2002 World Cup Games has been newly constructed at Sangam-dong in western Seoul.

The Main Stadium for the 2002 World Cup Games has a special design in the form of a kite and a sail which has been adopted to reveal Korean traditional beauty.

205

The Cheer Leader Group for the 2002 World Cup Games is called the "Red Devils." The cheer leaders wear the uniform of the soccer players. They lead the cheering group to encourage the soccer players.

ABOUT THE AUTHOR

Photograph by Cho Jae-Hee

Text and Photographs by Suh Jae-Sik

SUH JAE-SIK is a well known photographer who has published widely and has won a number of prestigious awards both nationally and internationally. In 1986, he was a photographer/ reporter for the Asian Games, and again in 1988 for the Olympic Games. For his remarkable photography, he received the "Prize from the Minister of Culture and Tourism" at the photography competition held under the auspices of the Korea National Tourism Organization. In addition, he has received more than 50 prizes at various photography competitions. He published *The Beauty of Korea* in 1998. In 1999, he was commissioned to work on the book, *HanOak : Traditional Korean Homes*. For his outstanding work, he received the "Hankuk Baeksang Publishing Culture Grand Prix" that was conferred by the Hankuk Ilbo Daily Newspaper.

Mr. Suh worked as a photographer for *Hanguk Hwabo* and magazine *Seoul*. Recently, his photographs can be seen in *Sweet Place for Living*, a magazine published by Goyang City. He was also the photographer of the internationally well-known book, *The Spirit of Korea Taekwondo*. Currently he is working on *The Thirty-Year History of Pohang Steel*. Mr. Suh, a member of the Korea Photographer's Association, is an outstanding photographer who has greatly influenced the field of photography in Korea.

Address : 521-201 Jugong APT, 131 Sangil-dong, Gangdong-gu, Seoul, Korea

Telephone : (02)442-8084   Cellular phone: 011-891-8088

E-mail : sjaesik@hanmail.net

DATE DUE

DEMCO, INC. 38-2931